# Trompe l'Oeil Stenciling

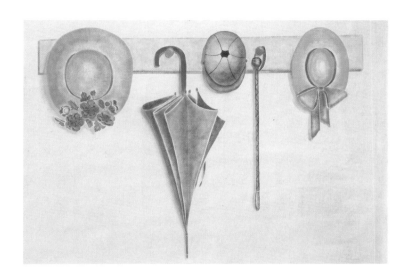

*In memory of my mother, who taught me perseverance in work and to aim high.*

I would like to thank my colleagues of *English Home* for their artistic collaboration;
Cristina for transforming classic designs into three-dimensional borders;
Paolo for his creations: the lobster, the shells, the fruit bowl, still life, cherries, pears, and "potiche";
Paola Fantin for the bowl of lemons and the candleholder.

10  9  8  7  6  5  4  3  2  1

First paperback edition published in 2001 by
Sterling Publishing Company, Inc.
387 Park Avenue South, New York, N.Y. 10016
First published in Italy by RCS Libri S.p.A.
Under the title *Trompe l'Oeil*
© 1999 by RCS Libri S.p.A.
English translation © 2000 by Sterling Publishing Company, Inc.
Distributed in Canada by Sterling Publishing
℅ Canadian Manda Group, One Atlantic Avenue, Suite 105
Toronto, Ontario, Canada M6K 3E7
Distributed in Great Britain and Europe by Cassell PLC
Wellington House, 125 Strand, London WC2R 0BB, England
Distributed in Australia by Capricorn Link (Australia) Pty Ltd.
P.O. Box 6651, Baulkham Hills, Business Centre, NSW 2153, Australia

Sterling ISBN 0-8069-2851-4 Trade
          0-8069-2852-2 Paper

Jocelyn Kerr Holding

# Trompe l'Oeil Stenciling

Sterling Publishing Co., Inc.
New York

# TABLE OF CONTENTS

PREFACE................................. 6

TIPS ON TECHNIQUE....................... 8

MATERIALS NEEDED...................... 11

## STENCILS WITH BRIDGES...... 13

CUTTING STENCILS WITH BRIDGES........... 14

COLORING STENCILS WITH BRIDGES......... 16

ISOLATING THE VARIOUS ELEMENTS ......... 18

USE OF ISOLATED ELEMENTS IN INTERIOR
DECORATING................................ 20

RETOUCHING BRIDGES...................... 22
Daffodils................................. 23
Bluebells................................. 24
Pansies .................................. 25

## MULTI-STEP STENCILING................... 27

MAKING A DOUBLE-STEP STENCIL........... 28

COLORING A DOUBLE-STEP STENCIL ........ 30

MAKING A GARLAND....................... 32

COLORING A FOUR-STEP STENCIL ........... 34

## PROJECTS.......................... 37

LIGHT AND SHADE ......................... 38
The fan.................................. 39
A bottle................................. 40
A satin shoe............................. 41

RAMAGE. . . . . . . . . . . . . . . . . . . . . . . . . . . . 42
The rose vine. . . . . . . . . . . . . . . . . . . . . . . . . 42
The theorem rose . . . . . . . . . . . . . . . . . . . . . . 44
Ivy. . . . . . . . . . . . . . . . . . . . . . . . . . . . . . . . . 48
Grapes. . . . . . . . . . . . . . . . . . . . . . . . . . . . . . 50

ANIMAL PORTRAITS. . . . . . . . . . . . . . . . . . . 52
Dogs . . . . . . . . . . . . . . . . . . . . . . . . . . . . . . . 52
Cats. . . . . . . . . . . . . . . . . . . . . . . . . . . . . . . . 53

# 3D STENCILING . . . . . . . . . . . . . . . . . . . . . 55

MAKING A 3D STENCIL . . . . . . . . . . . . . . . . 56
Still life. . . . . . . . . . . . . . . . . . . . . . . . . . . . . . 57
The shelf. . . . . . . . . . . . . . . . . . . . . . . . . . . . . 58
Transparent objects . . . . . . . . . . . . . . . . . . . 62
The fruit bowl . . . . . . . . . . . . . . . . . . . . . . . . 64
The candle . . . . . . . . . . . . . . . . . . . . . . . . . . 66
The glass and jug. . . . . . . . . . . . . . . . . . . . . 68
Fried eggs and French bread . . . . . . . . . . . . 70
Lemons. . . . . . . . . . . . . . . . . . . . . . . . . . . . . 72
Shells and lobster . . . . . . . . . . . . . . . . . . . . 74
Pears and cherries . . . . . . . . . . . . . . . . . . . 78
Tray with lace and rose decorations. . . . . . . 80
Vase with flowers. . . . . . . . . . . . . . . . . . . . . 82

SHADES. . . . . . . . . . . . . . . . . . . . . . . . . . . . 84
Rhombi box . . . . . . . . . . . . . . . . . . . . . . . . . 86

CREATING VOLUME AND SPACE . . . . . . . . . . .88
A bookcase frame . . . . . . . . . . . . . . . . . . . . .90
Books. . . . . . . . . . . . . . . . . . . . . . . . . . . . . . .92
A traditional vase. . . . . . . . . . . . . . . . . . . . . 94
Wall lamp and candleholder. . . . . . . . . . . . . 96
Pewter goblets and plates . . . . . . . . . . . . . . 98
Clothes Hanger . . . . . . . . . . . . . . . . . . . . . 100
Straw hat with ribbon . . . . . . . . . . . . . . . . . 102
Riding cap and crop . . . . . . . . . . . . . . . . . . 104
An umbrella. . . . . . . . . . . . . . . . . . . . . . . . . 106
Chinese motifs. . . . . . . . . . . . . . . . . . . . . . 108
"Potiche" . . . . . . . . . . . . . . . . . . . . . . . . . . 108

ARCHITECTONIC MOTIFS. . . . . . . . . . . . . . . 110
The capital . . . . . . . . . . . . . . . . . . . . . . . . . 112
Victorian motif . . . . . . . . . . . . . . . . . . . . . . 111
The rose motif. . . . . . . . . . . . . . . . . . . . . . . 114

# STENCILS . . . . . . . . . . . . . . . . . . . 117

# INDEX . . . . . . . . . . . . . . . . . . 160

# PREFACE

Down through the centuries, the tradition of decorating the walls of one's home represented a veritable form of artistic expression. Today the stencil has earned its place among the classic decorative techniques. We all remember the delightful borders of flowers and fruit or the row of ducks splashing away on the bathroom tiles. The stencil has by now, however, moved towards a real art technique, the trompe l'oeil.

The trompe l'oeil or 3D stencil produces results of great interest even when compared to quite recent creations. To achieve this effect, the pictorial chiaroscuro technique is applied to the traditional stenciling method, while a special use is made of the stencil itself.

This manual offers a wide variety of decorations, compositions, and scenes, almost all of them explained step-by-step. Not everyone, of course, will achieve these effects at first go, but with time and patience success is ensured. Both enthusiasts and beginners will enter a new and unexplored world, one that will stimulate their imagination and, I am quite sure, thoroughly enchant them.

As with all trompe l'oeil scenes, those created with the help of stencils must follow the rules of perspective. The in-depth effect is obtained by means of the chiaroscuro technique. We shall learn to observe the source of light, as the position of the object with regard to light determines whether shading must be light, darker, or very dark. If the object is placed behind another, it will reflect its shadows; if instead it is in the background of the scene, its tones will be muted. With shading we can create an effect of volume on a curved surface: the part nearest to the point of observation is bright, whereas the parts of the scene that gradually fade into the distance are darker.

Furthermore, the traditional stencil technique is so easy that it can be learned in a few hours' lessons. Then, by carefully following certain rules, you can also express your creativity through the magical world of the trompe l'oeil stencil.

*Jocelyn Kerr Holding*

# TIPS ON TECHNIQUE

Those already familiar with stencil work know that to obtain sharp outlines and even, compact coloring it is essential to use fast-drying colors such as acrylics, in very small, non-diluted portions.

The stencil brush must be used with a circular stroke: by pressing harder, more color is spread and dark nuances are created.

Where the choice is for solid colors in the stick form or for creams, painting is carried out in the same way. Care must be taken, however, against smudging, as these colors, being oil-based, do not dry at once as do acrylics, but remain damp for at least ten minutes. Backed by my personal experience, I hold that acrylic colors give the best results, both with regard to application and to shading.

I also wish to recommend a product extremely useful to have at hand when working for a long period with the same brush: the retarding medium for acrylics. This substance restores softness to the brush, thus allowing the color to be spread with greater fluidness. A small phial of retarding medium will also turn out to be indispensable when working out of doors, or in

warm surroundings, where the color could dry quickly, hardening the brush bristles. Having dipped the brush into the color and passed it over a paper towel, all is ready to begin coloring the stencil. This is a useful operation both for getting rid of excess color and for spreading it out well over the bristles. Paint with circular strokes in both directions. For a "Ferrara"-type border the result will be stunning if shaded in two or more colors. Begin with the lightest color without filling in the whole design, then follow with the intermediate tones and finish with the darkest color. A section of this manual is given over to shading and nuancing techniques and will explain how to obtain chiaroscuro effects. Information is furthermore given on how to achieve three-dimensional effects and the optical illusion of movement in the borders.

# MATERIALS NEEDED

## COLORS

My longtime experience in pictorial technique and practice has helped me to get to know the many and varied assortment of materials and colors available on the market, from the oil-based stick to the sponge dipped in ink and to oil colors for artists. But not one of these materials ever persuaded me as much as did acrylic colors in the form of liquid cream, ideal for obtaining an even, smearless effect.

Acrylic colors, in fact, contain synthetic resin and therefore dry quickly – an absolutely essential characteristic when doing multi-step work. They are used for wall, wood, rough terra-cotta, and all other porous and rigid surfaces.

For stenciling on fabric, use colors specifically designed for this purpose, but make sure first of all that the fabric is made of natural fibers. Having finished the design, wait 12 hours and then iron with a hot iron without steam, so as to make the colors fast. Thereafter the article may be washed in the washing machine even up to 60° C. Should you wish to paint on pottery, use unprepared colors for pottery (solvent-based colors in great variety can be found). Some of these colors have to be fired in the home oven for about 5 minutes at 80° C with the oven door open. When finished, the stenciled object may easily be hand-washed with liquid soap and water.

## THE RETARDING MEDIUM

This is a glycol oil-based medium, a product compatible with acrylic colors. As already mentioned, it is used when working in warm surroundings or out of doors, when acrylics tend to dry too quickly and the brush becomes rigid, thus preventing the circular strokes that are essential for obtaining good results. A few drops of medium on the brush does the trick, and the color becomes fluid once more.

## BRUSHES

Stencil brushes must be very flexible so as to regulate hand pressure to the shading desired. Essential shading strokes require long, soft bristles. Brushes with short or too hard bristles are unsuitable.

## ROLLERS

When a multi-step stencil is used to create a 3D border, it's a good idea to employ a roller instead of a stencil brush. In this case there is no need to shade, for what is wanted is an even spread. The 3D effect is the result of different tonalities.

Acrylic colors may also be used with the roller, and the method is the same. Having dipped the roller in the paint, the excess color is eliminated on paper towel so as to avoid smudging.

## MYLAR

This is a polyester extract. It is very scratch-resistant and indestructible if preserved well. Mylar stencils must be cleaned well after use with warm water and liquid soap.

As an alternative, stencil film may be used, but this is much less resistant.

## PAPER ADHESIVE

This is needed to affix the stencil to the surface. Should the surface have mobile parts, the use of a repositionable spray is advised.

## CUTTER

The cutter allows precise, easy incision. Cut your stencil on a glass surface; this greatly helps you make clean, sharp incision.

# STENCILS WITH BRIDGES

# CUTTING STENCILS WITH BRIDGES

Stencils must be cut with a firm, decisive hand. Always cut towards you, making sure that your working surface is hard and will not yield to pressure from the knife.

Glass makes the ideal base since it is extremely hard and transparent. Place your design under the glass and your sheet of Mylar on it and proceed to trace the outlines. Guide the knife with your index finger and regulate the pressure of your hand.

When transforming a design into a stencil, remember that it is not possible to cut just one element. For example, if an element is within a circle, it is either transposed to another stencil or else, during cutting, bridges are left to unite it to the rest of the design. The specific role of bridges therefore is to keep the various parts together. Bridges are made up of narrow strips of film that divide the various design elements.

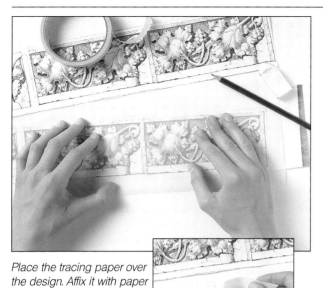

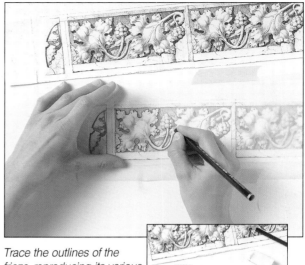

Place the tracing paper over the design. Affix it with paper adhesive.

Trace the outlines of the frieze, reproducing its various elements.

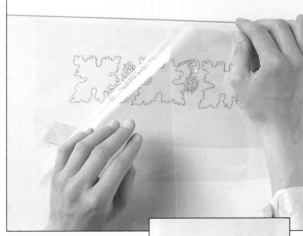

Repeat the design, dividing it into elements and adding the bridges.

Place the design – now become a stencil – under a glass surface onto which transparent film has been attached. Cut through the film with a sharp cutter.

# COLORING STENCILS WITH BRIDGES

Through correct shading, even a small stencil with bridges can be transformed  into a 3D frieze. "Lotus" is a typical example. The two ends of the design present an elongated, rounded shape. By sharply outlining the outer edge and only lightly shading the center, the rounded part takes on an ovular form.

Care in using the brush is necessary when regulating pressure in order to obtain lighter and darker parts, thus employing the chiaroscuro technique. When using more than one color, begin with the lighter and then overlay the darker. The transparent color effect achieved is very pleasing. By darkening instead all the parts characterizing the shape of the design – e.g., the tip of the leaves or a twirl that ends off a frieze – the line is highlighted and an effect of movement created.

## LOTUS

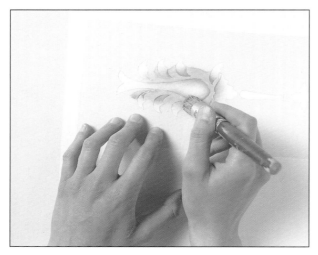

*Dip the stencil brush in the color, then pass it over a paper towel to get rid of any excess paint. With a circular movement, begin painting the stencil, working from the outside inwards.*

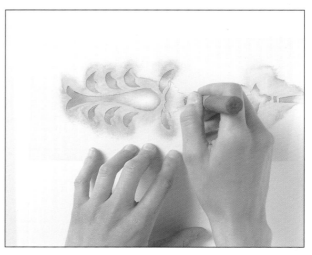

*Where the design is slightly rounded, leave the center part a lighter color, so as to achieve an effect of volume (or 3D).*

# EAGLE

The borders that we here propose as "Eagle" are usually used to decorate boxes, wardrobe panels, or visiting cards, or as simple borders for walls. A characteristic of stencil friezes is that they create rhythm and movement in an anonymous, bare environment.

# STAR

A small star motif can become the main decoration for bathroom tiles or, reproduced in sequence, turn into a border that gives personality to a room or a furnishing element or an object.

# ISOLATING THE VARIOUS ELEMENTS

Stencils depicting old friezes offer an incredible wealth of decorating elements. By isolating a detail of a frieze it is possible to create an endless variety of artistic borders. This technique is particularly suitable for interior decorating.

*Rovigo*

*Liberty*

*Lotus*

*Padova*

# VERONA

The stencil obtained by tracing this frieze – originally a bas-relief on an eighteenth-century door – is well suited to being divided up into various elements. This isolating of the various elements in the "Verona" stencil has given rise to another four borders: Liberty, Lotus, Padova, and Rovigo.

# USE OF ISOLATED ELEMENTS IN INTERIOR DECORATING

*Further separated elements have been used to decorate the walls under this ceiling cornice and, in a larger version, along the skirting board and around a door, thus creating a pleasant idea of movement.*

*The examples proposed on these pages are isolated elements of the "Perugia" stencil. One element decorates the wall under the ceiling cornice and contours the door; the other has been used to frame the borders of a sideboard.*

The "Verona" frieze was chosen to decorate this carpet, entirely stenciled. This composition, divided in half, was used to form a frieze high up under the ceiling.

This border, seen against the warm rose color of the walls, creates an extremely cozy and inviting atmosphere.

# RETOUCHING BRIDGES

When using a stenciled design, it is not always possible to do without bridges or create motifs with more than one stencil. Flowers in particular, with their often complicated shapes, fall into this category. To make them, we therefore need bridges, which are later eliminated.

# DAFFODILS

Using a fine brush (0), fill in the space between the petals in very light yellow. Then darken the outer part of the corolla with the slightly darker yellow.

Position the stencil on the flower once more and, dabbing with the stencil brush, touch up the outer petals and flower base with burnt sienna. Add the green parts to hide the bridges.

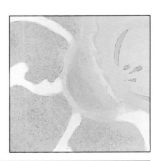

# BLUEBELLS

With a fine brush and using the dark blue color of the center of the flower, highlight the dark line that divides the petals. Lightly shade the middle of the flower – always using a fine pen.

Discard the bridges used for the green parts of the vine.

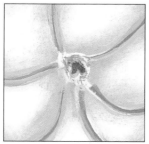
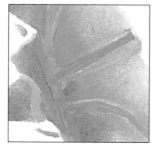
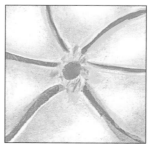

# PANSIES

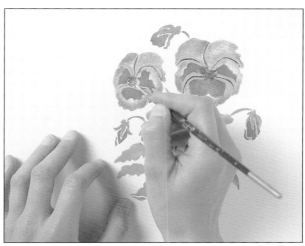

*Reposition the petals so as to fill in the space left by the bridge.*

*The dark violet lines will thus be finer and the flower divided into various parts. Finish off by retouching the leaves and the buds.*

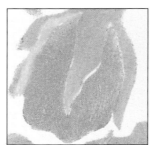

# MULTI-STEP
# STENCILING

# MAKING A DOUBLE-STEP STENCIL

Multi-step stenciling allows us to eliminate bridges by separating colors. Usually the first working step concerns the composition of the design, while the details are added later. Where designs with superimposed motifs are involved, two stencils must necessarily be made in order to reproduce the design faithfully.

## SPOLETO

*Apply the tracing paper to the chosen motif and trace the outlines.*

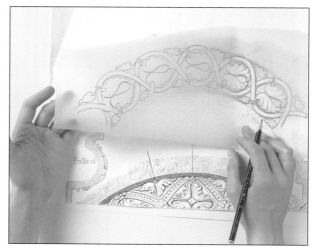

*Carefully detach the tracing paper, which will act as a trace for cutting out the first stencil.*

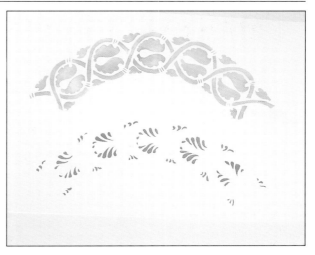

On another sheet of paper, trace the details that will underline the shaded parts once the second stencil has been cut.

Begin coloring, using a light tone. Proceed then to the second step with a darker color for the shadows.

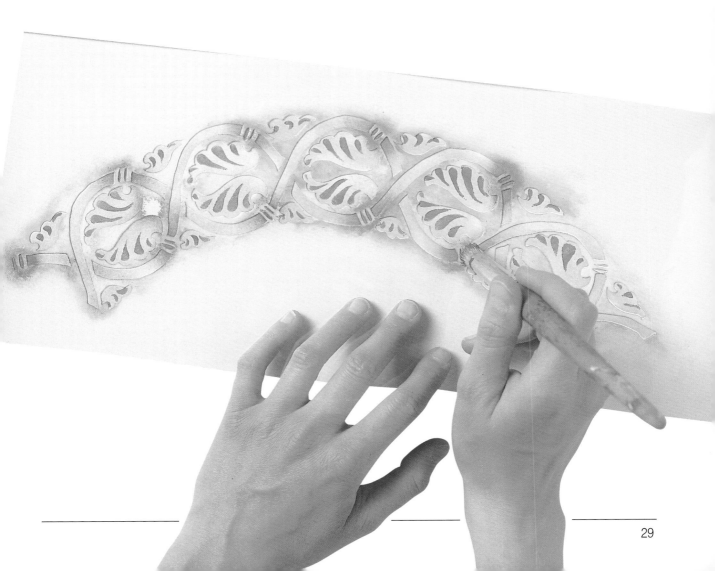

# COLORING A DOUBLE-STEP STENCIL

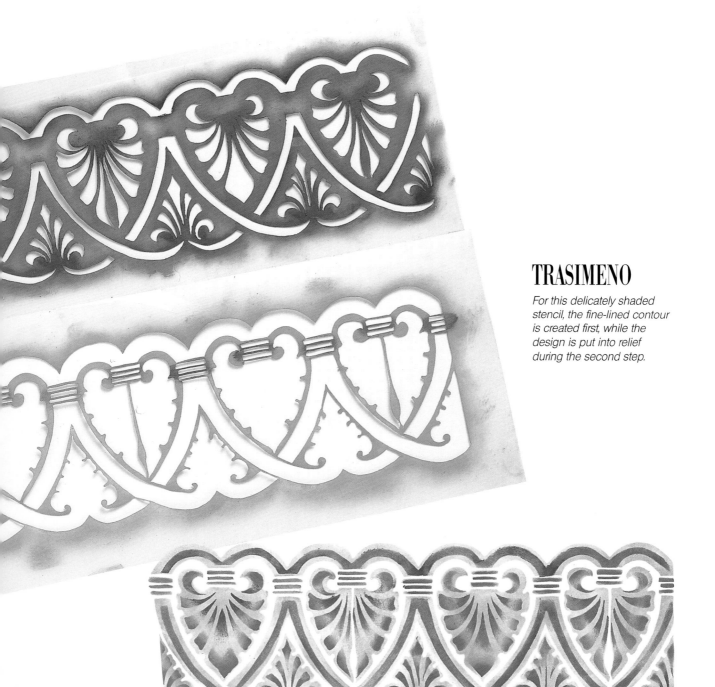

## TRASIMENO

*For this delicately shaded stencil, the fine-lined contour is created first, while the design is put into relief during the second step.*

# BAROQUE

For the corner motif, choose two shades of color, one slightly darker than the other.

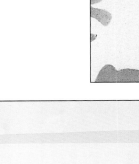

Use the darker tone for the parts that are to appear shaded.

Overlay the second stencil and apply the lighter color.

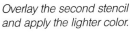

When the corner border is finished, continue to position the border stencil, alternating the two shades of color.

# MAKING A GARLAND

With a curved stencil such as "Spoleto" or "Siracusa" it is possible to obtain a beautiful garland both as a frame for a picture and for a rose window motif around a source of light. To prepare the stencil, a circle of the desired size must be drawn and divided into segments. The size of the stencil must be equal to the circumference section of the segment.

## SIRACUSA

*Only a part of this garland is stenciled. Beginning with a circle, continue by drawing the motif freehand. In this double-step motif, the light and dark nuances are equal.*

*Draw a circle with a big compass or simply use a drawing pin, a piece of twine and a pencil. Divide the circle into segments.*

*Cut the stencil to size and place it on the circumference. Color it with two shades of the same color.*

Detach the stencil and reposition it, making it fit the design accurately. Attach with paper adhesive and hide the part that protrudes beyond the segment.

Continue positioning the stencil and coloring in two shades, until a perfect garland has been obtained.

# COLORING A FOUR-STEP STENCIL

With a four-step stencil, it is possible to create a 3D impression through the clever use of the chiaroscuro technique, which highlights the lighting contrasts reflected on the object. In the case of an architectonic element in very pronounced relief, the contrasts between light and shade show up by the alternating of light, lighter, and very dark zones. The 3D borders shown here in detail are lit from the left. As a consequence, the light points are highlighted on the left of all the elements making up the design, while the right side shows shadows in various nuances of chiaroscuro.

*Prepare the four color shades, ranging from lighter to darker. Mark the reference points indicated on each stencil, because they are essential for repositioning during the subsequent steps.*

*Dip the roller in the first color, then pass it over paper towel.*

*Affix the first-step stencil to the wall with paper adhesive and begin coloring with the roller.*

*Position the second-step stencil, bearing the reference points in mind. Apply the second color with a uniform movement.*

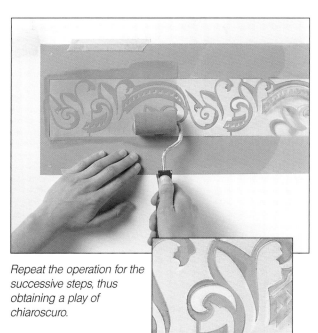

*Repeat the operation for the successive steps, thus obtaining a play of chiaroscuro.*

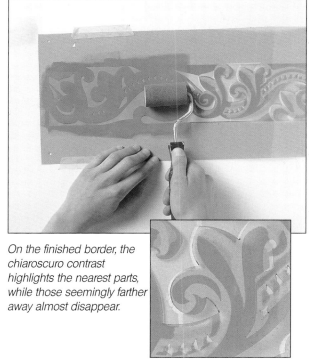

*On the finished border, the chiaroscuro contrast highlights the nearest parts, while those seemingly farther away almost disappear.*

# PROJECTS

# LIGHT AND SHADE

A play of light and shade is essential in order to obtain a 3D effect. To study the reflection of light on an object and the variety of nuances that the source of light (solar or artificial) creates, it is enough to observe it carefully and closely. Having analyzed the outline of the shadows, one can pass on to applying the trompe l'oeil.

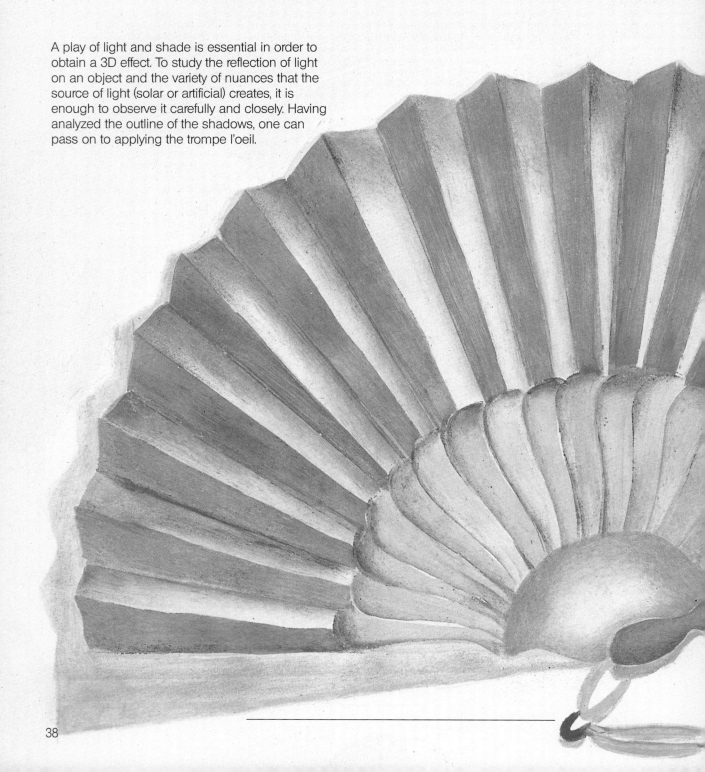

## THE FAN

The pleats of the fan represent a good example of chiaroscuro. The light in this case illuminates the object from the right. Six stencils are necessary to make this fan, one for all the light colored strips of the pleat, and another for all the dark ones; two for the semi-circle, one for the green wooden support and one for the silk cords and the tassels.

# A BOTTLE

*The cork is shown shading on its left side. As it is made up of a smaller cylinder than the bottle, the strongest shadow is seen on the left side, leaving a small beam of bright light in the center.*

*The illumination is directed towards the front, a little to the right, while a slight shading on the left side extends over half the bottle. On the right side a sharp, dark shading outlines the contours and continues, gradually fading, as far as the central part, where it dissolves in a ray of white light.*

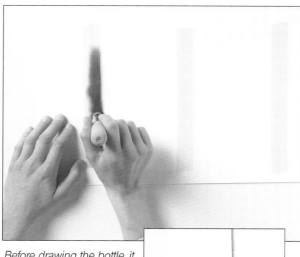

*Before drawing the bottle, it is a good idea to practice the shading technique. Shading is made with a sharp, very dark line corresponding to the darkest shaded point and is obtained by covering with paper adhesive the part which is to remain bright.*

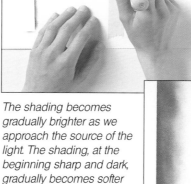

*The shading becomes gradually brighter as we approach the source of the light. The shading, at the beginning sharp and dark, gradually becomes softer until it disappears.*

# A SATIN SHOE

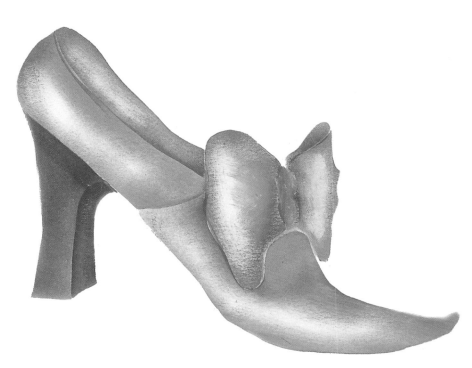

This satin shoe with a bow is made with simple elements placed together. Its shape and the grain of the fabric are highlighted by careful shading. The shoe shows a beam of light where the shape is rounded. The bow, lit from the left, is whitish at the sides and dark green in the center. The heel is painted in two shades of brown, the darker shade being used to create the inside shadow.

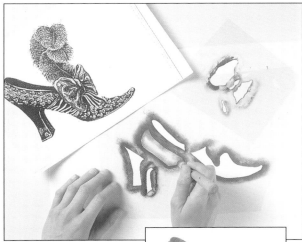

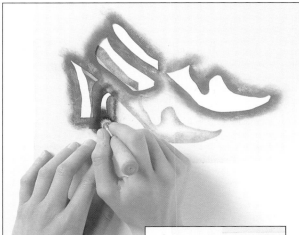

Position the stencil and shade the curved-back part of the shoe. Paint the front part and shade it lightly. Position the stencil for the heel and color, using a not too dark tone.

Now begin painting the inside of the heel, coloring it in a decidedly darker shade. Position and color the bow stencil, shading it with a lighter tone at the ends and leaving a white line in the middle.

# RAMAGE

Ramage is formed by a succession of elements placed one beside the other to give the effect of a growing plant. One leaf is placed after another, a branch is positioned in the distance and another in the foreground and in this way the composition acquires perspective. With a multi-step stencil it is possible to create volume, eliminating bridges and obtaining a trompe l'oeil effect.
At the end of the work, leaves and stems are retouched freehand, joining all and creating the leaf veins.

## THE ROSE VINE

*Using the multi-stencil technique we can make this vine of roses and clematis. The branches are added at the end of the work freehand, with the use of a fine brush.*

# THE THEOREM ROSE

Flowers make an ideal subject for trompe l'oeil stenciling. The petals are delicately shaded, darker where they join other petals, light where they curve. The leaves are overlaid, creating a play of light and shade contrasts. The veins are added by hand or with a small stencil. All the parts must fit perfectly together to make up the flower.

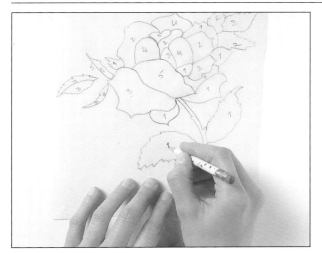

Before cutting the stencil, it is necessary to divide the elements of the rose in six parts that correspond to the six stencils. The elements on each individual stencil are not to be touched.

Position the stencil, making a reference point for the succeeding steps. Lightly color each detail of the stencil, working from the outside inwards.

Position the second stencil, keeping the design in mind and, having overlaid it on the already marked reference points, proceed with the coloring.

Position the third stencil and outline the petals, highlighting the shading in the overlaid points.

*Position the fourth stencil. The rose is now almost complete. Shade the leaves to make them as natural as possible.*

*Complete the composition with the last stencil. The final petal will be of a more intense color at the base, almost white where it curves and again dark along the outlines.*

The veins of the leaves are achieved with the covering stencils in Mylar, placed perpendicular to the central veins. In this example, the light that is reflected on the petals and on the leaves comes from the left. While working, pay close attention to the source of light; it must be coming from one sole direction.

# IVY

Nothing is so right for this composition as a creeper. Of these the most classical is without doubt the climbing ivy, thanks to the intertwining and overlapping of its characteristic green-shot leaves. The composition may be achieved with just one stencil or by combining various parts. The shading along the branches and the leaves helps give the idea of movement and growth to the plant. It must always be carried out on the same side, according to the source of the light.

Position the stencil and paint the ivy vine. Finish the bigger leaves with dark green veining by hand with a fine brush.

Light green is used, instead, for the veining of the smaller leaves. Touch up the branches freehand so as to avoid mistakes.

Shading must always take into account the source of light, which here comes from the left. On the right, a slight tint of gray outlines the composition.

# GRAPES

These seemingly three-dimensional grapes differ from traditional stenciled grapes in that each individual grape is here overlapped in an extremely realistic manner. The bunches are not difficult to make if covering stencils are used to protect the parts already colored.

Draw the outline of the bunch freehand and then fill in the grapes, the vine, and the leaves.

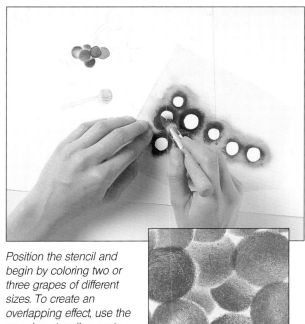

Position the stencil and begin by coloring two or three grapes of different sizes. To create an overlapping effect, use the covering stencil so as to color only the figure in the foreground. Paint with different tones of the same color, or colors belonging to the same range.

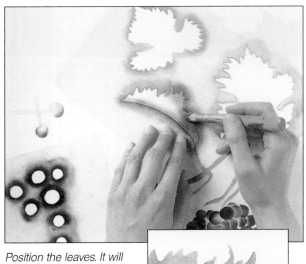

Position the leaves. It will sometimes be necessary to use the negative part of the stencil to cover the elements already colored.

The finished bunch will present darker and lighter grapes, depending on their position with regard to the source of light. Complete the ramage by varying the shadings, particularly on the leaves and the vine.

# ANIMAL PORTRAITS

## DOGS

With trompe-l'oeil stencil you can make a portrait of your pet dog. This dog was made by using various stencils; the colors used were dark brown mixed with ochre and burnt sienna. Prepare one stencil for the outline and another for the face. The snout effect is achieved by darkening it lengthwise and just under the nostrils, leaving the higher portion a lighter shade. The nose tip is obtained by using three overlaid stencils. A sharp dark line divides the head and body. A few freehand strokes will help make the eyes and mouth more expressive.

# CATS

Transfer the cat outline using a stencil. Different stencils then create the head, body, tail, stripes, eyes, nose, and mouth. Highlight the head and tail with darker shading where the stencils meet. Touch up the eyes, nose, mouth, and whiskers by hand.

# 3D STENCILING

# MAKING A 3D STENCIL

The stenciling technique, both artistic and creative, is in constant evolution. Stenciling, in fact, was once achieved through the repetition of 2D motifs, and used to decorate walls and other architectonic elements, the volumetric effect being obtained by color changes. 3D stencils create the three-dimensional effect by isolating various elements of the original design into different stencils; this permits a more simple use of the trompe-l'oeil technique.

The end result depends on individual skill in using colors and applying freehand finishing touches.

These stencils also make it possible to vary composition shapes at will. The 3D effect, however, can only be achieved by the correct use of the chiaroscuro techniques and the laws of perspective.

# STILL LIFE

In this stencil copy of a painting by a seventeeth-century Dutch artist, we find the subtle charm of a still life, with its meticulous reproduction of the various objects and its play of chiaroscuro. To reproduce it, first prepare the stencils necessary for the composition. Then make the copy of the still life, following the layout of the various elements.
Once you've finished stenciling, fill in the blank spaces with a small brush and create some shading on the fruit.

# THE SHELF

The effect of depth in this shelf was obtained by coloring the space between two strips of adhesive tape placed on the wall with two shades of brown. The lower part of the shelf was drawn bearing in mind the flight point of perspective, which in this case is central. The plates, teapot and cups were, instead, created by using various stencils, volume being given through color modulation.

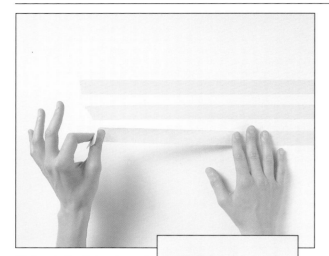

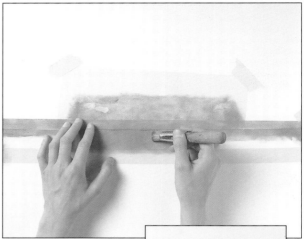

Delineate the flat surface of the shelf with three strips of adhesive tape, and color with a light shade of brown.

Divide the two strips of color with a dark line to create depth. Cover the top part of the flat surface with transparent film and deepen the color to obtain the shading between the top and bottom parts of the shelf.

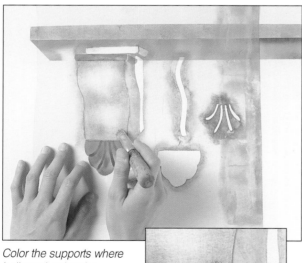

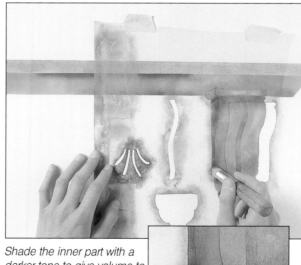

Color the supports where indicated, using the appropriate stencils.

Shade the inner part with a darker tone to give volume to the supports.

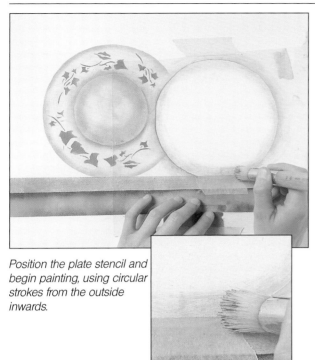

Position the plate stencil and begin painting, using circular strokes from the outside inwards.

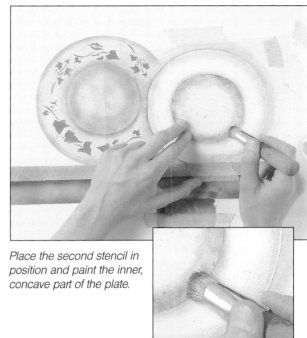

Place the second stencil in position and paint the inner, concave part of the plate.

Shade the edge of the plate with a terra-cotta tint. Position the ivy stencil and color the ramage, being careful to use the darker tone of brown.

Detach the stencil with care and leave the work to dry.

# TRANSPARENT OBJECTS

*Depicted here is a fruit arrangement in a crystal bowl, the fruit placed in a very natural fashion. To make this arrangement, great attention must be paid to the proportions of the fruit visible through the bowl and of that overhanging it. Note the direction of the light before beginning to color, so as to shade the composition properly.*

# THE FRUIT BOWL

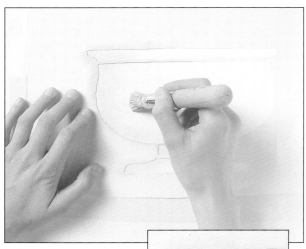

This arrangement calls for a new method of procedure that results in an effect of transparent glass. Mix the pale blue and white colors together and dilute the mixture with water and a drop of retarder medium. Place the stencil in position and paint from the outside inwards. Put no pressure on the brush, because the color must turn out very light.

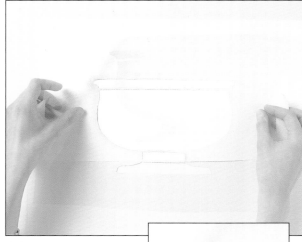

Color the entire bowl, remembering to work with circular strokes and only the slightest pressure. Pass the same color once more over the sides to create roundness.
Detach the stencil and put the finishing touches freehand to eliminate any imperfections. It is advisable to try this out first on cardboard to avoid ruining the arrangement.

Trace the bowl outline with a pencil, then draw the fruit, endeavoring to arrange it as naturally as possible.

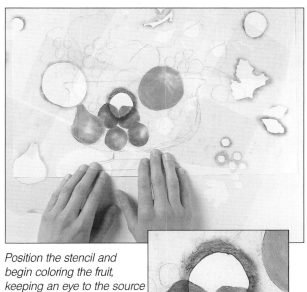

Position the stencil and begin coloring the fruit, keeping an eye to the source of light. Use covering stencils to protect the already painted fruit, over which the other elements of the composition will be superimposed.

Shade the fruit, keeping the shapes in mind and using a darker tone for cavities.

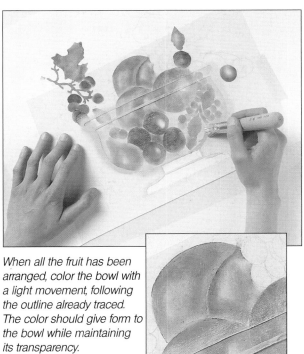

When all the fruit has been arranged, color the bowl with a light movement, following the outline already traced. The color should give form to the bowl while maintaining its transparency.

# THE CANDLE

Position the stencil for the base and color. Shade with a darker color near the point of support, and leave the center part white to highlight its roundness. Place the first candle support section near the base.

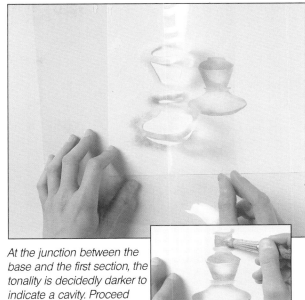

At the junction between the base and the first section, the tonality is decidedly darker to indicate a cavity. Proceed with the second section, adding some light shading on the right side, which is in the path of the light.

Apply the color lightly along the two sides of the candle, leaving the centre light colored. Darken the right side of the candle to create shade.

Color the flame, dark at the base and light at the top. The falling wax should be darker near the candle.

# THE GLASS AND JUG

Initially, outline the whole glass with a slight touch of color. Over this place the first stencil for the wine and color with a hint of burgundy tone. Add the second stencil and heighten the color of the wine.

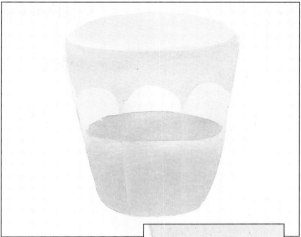

Insert an oval stencil to give depth to the glass and color. Superimpose the last stencil to create an arched effect on the glass, and paint with a darker tint.

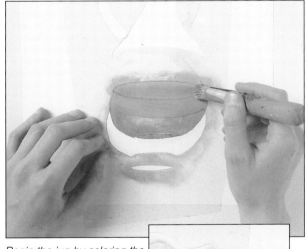

Begin the jug by coloring the wine contained in the lower part. Then paint with the second wine stencil, using a darker shading to give volume to the composition.

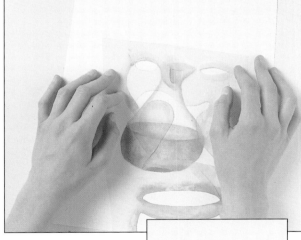

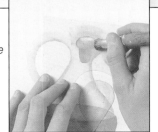

Proceed with the upper part of the jug, darkening slightly where there is a cavity. Place the lower part of the cork in position and color lightly. Finish off the upper part of the cork, shading the outer part with a darker tone and the center with a lighter one.

# FRIED EGGS AND FRENCH BREAD

*Color the pan, leaving the center white. To make the eggs, use the oval stencil in various positions, alternating shades of light and dark pink.*

*With an oval shape, color the egg nearest to you and color the eggs behind in very light pink.*

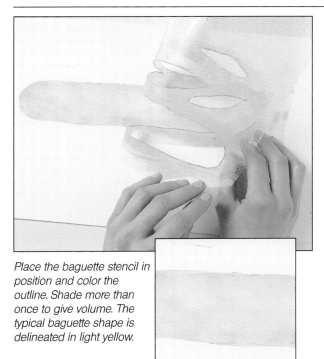

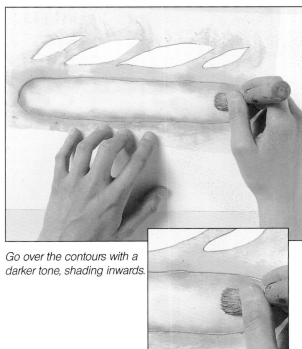

Place the baguette stencil in position and color the outline. Shade more than once to give volume. The typical baguette shape is delineated in light yellow.

Go over the contours with a darker tone, shading inwards.

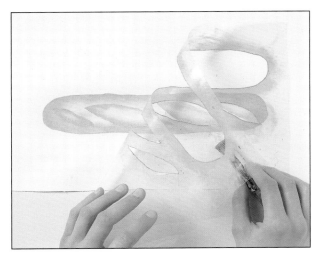

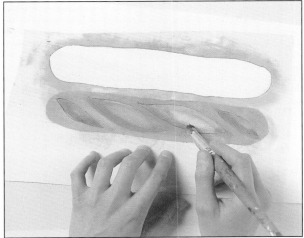

Position the stencils for the cuts typically worked into this bread, and cover with a medium-dark tint, leaving the center light colored.

With a dark tone, highlight the shading on the left and under the cuts.

# LEMONS

*Depicted here is a bowl of lemons and other fruits. It is not difficult to make: the fruits are made by matching and overlaying various stencils. The dark green shades highlight the line of the fruits, giving them volume.*

# SHELLS AND LOBSTER

Happy fish, sailing boats, and sailors' knots are the most popular subjects for decorating the walls of a house that is near the sea. Displayed on this page are a series of shells, jazzed up by the presence of a lovely red lobster. The shadows cleverly placed next to each object give the overall composition a 3D effect.

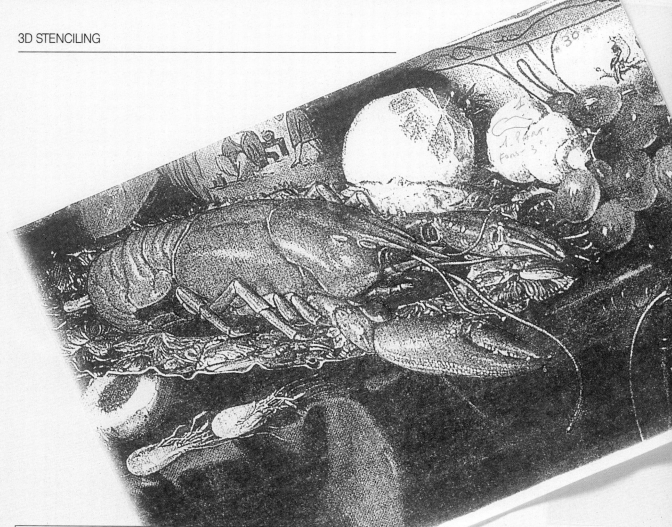

Photocopy the shells and cut out the stencils, two per object, one for the outline, which is then colored in light tones, the other for shading.

Photocopy the picture of a
lobster and divide it into
different stencils, one for the
body, one for the claws, and
two for the shading. The
details and nuancing are
done freehand.

# PEARS AND CHERRIES

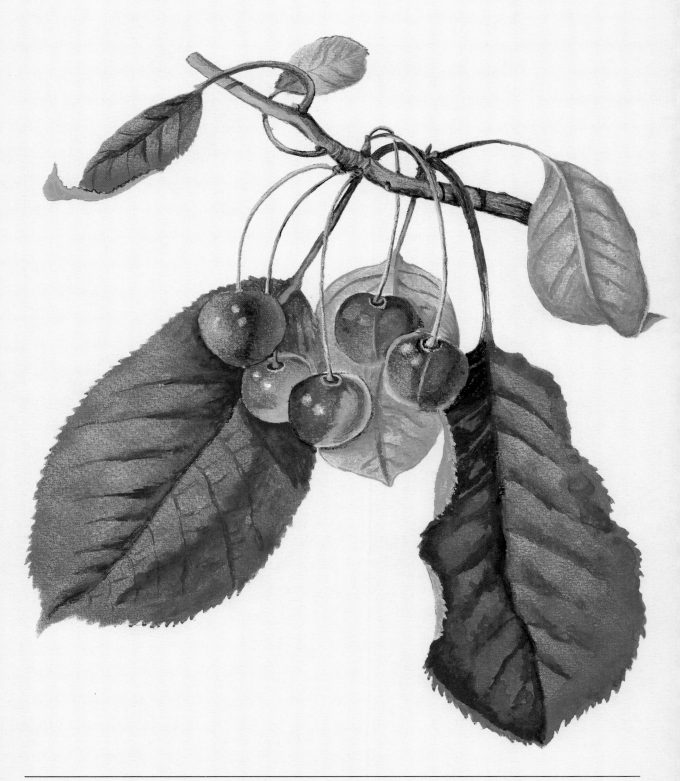

*Depicted on these pages are two examples of fruit made with multi-component stencils. The shading was achieved with a light touch of color. The veins of the leaves and the finishing touches were done freehand, using a fine brush.*

# TRAY WITH LACE AND ROSE DECORATIONS

This is a delicate decoration that can be reproduced on the surface of a table or a tray.

Paint the surface of the tray (a metal tray would be preferable) with white spray varnish. Leave to dry. Affix the stencil with the repositionable spray and paint the tray with matt black spray varnish. Once completely dry, remove the stencil.

To decorate, position the different rose stencils, beginning with the stem and leaf. Color using pre-prepared pottery colors. Leave to dry thoroughly. Position the flower and bud stencils, and then finish off with the one for coloring inside the petal. Once completed, mark the veins of the leaves with a fine brush and a darker color. With a dark gray pre-prepared pottery color, create shades along the left side of the branch.

Give the decoration various coats of transparent spray paint for protection purposes.

# VASE WITH FLOWERS

This composition depicting tulips in a crystal vase was achieved through multi-step stenciling. The flowers were made using a stencil divided into two parts, one for the light shades and the other for the darker ones. The leaves and stems are made up of three parts. The cone-shaped base of the vase was achieved by mixing light gray with a small quantity of blue. Paint with a circular movement; avoiding pressure on the brush so as to obtain the transparent effect desired.
Finish by applying the tulip stems in the vase, again avoiding pressure on the brush.

*This decoration of cyclamen and lylium was also made with multi-step stenciling, sometimes mirrored.*
*The vase was painted only at the end, with the cyclamen leaves, which must show in the foreground, covered in Mylar film.*

# SHADES

*The shadows on these objects are projected by a light reflecting from the left.*

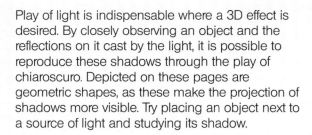

Play of light is indispensable where a 3D effect is desired. By closely observing an object and the reflections on it cast by the light, it is possible to reproduce these shadows through the play of chiaroscuro. Depicted on these pages are geometric shapes, as these make the projection of shadows more visible. Try placing an object next to a source of light and studying its shadow.

*On the right are the same objects with their shadows – this time, however, seen from above.*

# RHOMBI BOX

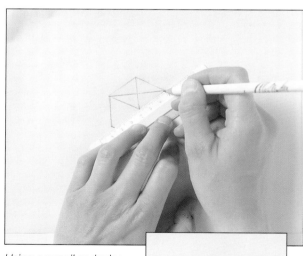

Using a pencil and ruler, draw a 2.5 cm cube. Reproduce it on tracing paper.

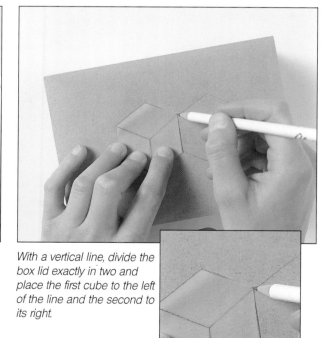

With a vertical line, divide the box lid exactly in two and place the first cube to the left of the line and the second to its right.

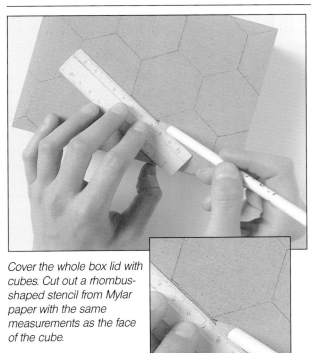

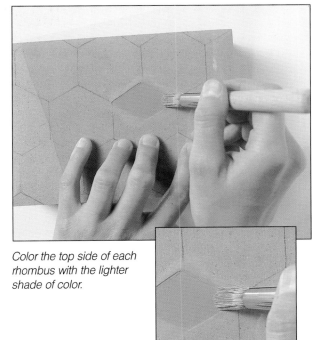

Cover the whole box lid with cubes. Cut out a rhombus-shaped stencil from Mylar paper with the same measurements as the face of the cube.

Color the top side of each rhombus with the lighter shade of color.

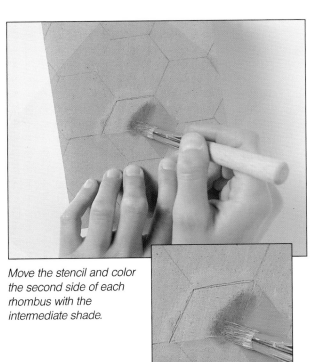

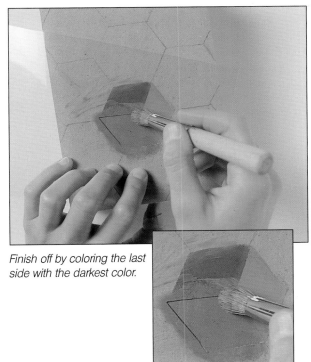

Move the stencil and color the second side of each rhombus with the intermediate shade.

Finish off by coloring the last side with the darkest color.

# CREATING VOLUME AND SPACE

With 3D stencilling, a higher standard of shading is achieved than that offered by the freehand trompe-l'oeil technique. This is evident in the two examples shown on the following pages, the library and the traditional vase, where shading is due to color gradation. It is advisable, however, to begin with objects that are not too difficult to make, for instance, a row of books on a shelf.

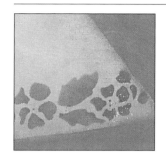

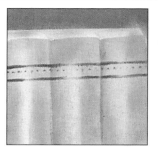

# A BOOKCASE FRAME

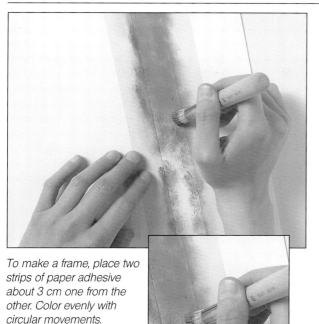

To make a frame, place two strips of paper adhesive about 3 cm one from the other. Color evenly with circular movements.

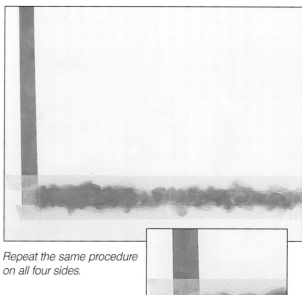

Repeat the same procedure on all four sides.

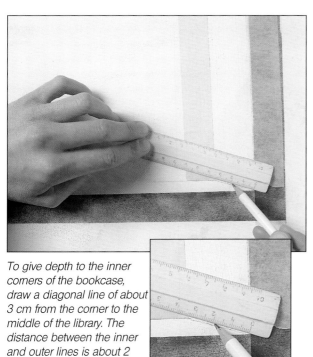

To give depth to the inner corners of the bookcase, draw a diagonal line of about 3 cm from the corner to the middle of the library. The distance between the inner and outer lines is about 2 cm. Repeat the same procedure for the remaining corners.

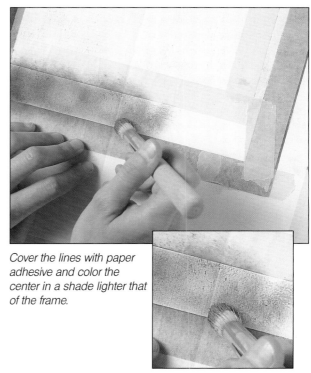

Cover the lines with paper adhesive and color the center in a shade lighter that of the frame.

# BOOKS

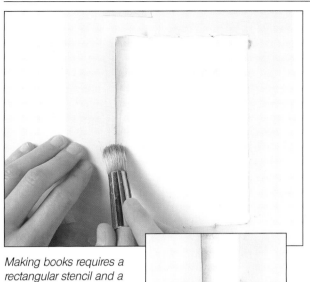

Making books requires a rectangular stencil and a strip of Mylar film to protect the parts already painted.

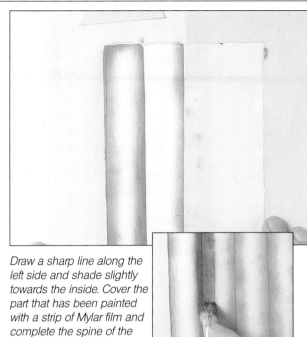

Draw a sharp line along the left side and shade slightly towards the inside. Cover the part that has been painted with a strip of Mylar film and complete the spine of the book.

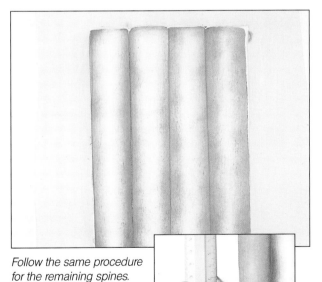

Follow the same procedure for the remaining spines. Make a 3 cm diagonal line, starting from the top corner of the spine of the last book, and a vertical line as far as the base to create the book cover.

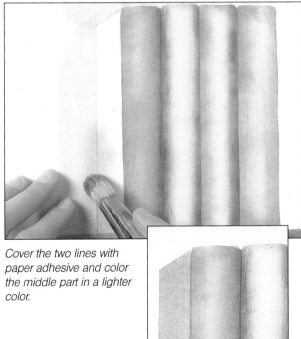

Cover the two lines with paper adhesive and color the middle part in a lighter color.

# A TRADITIONAL VASE

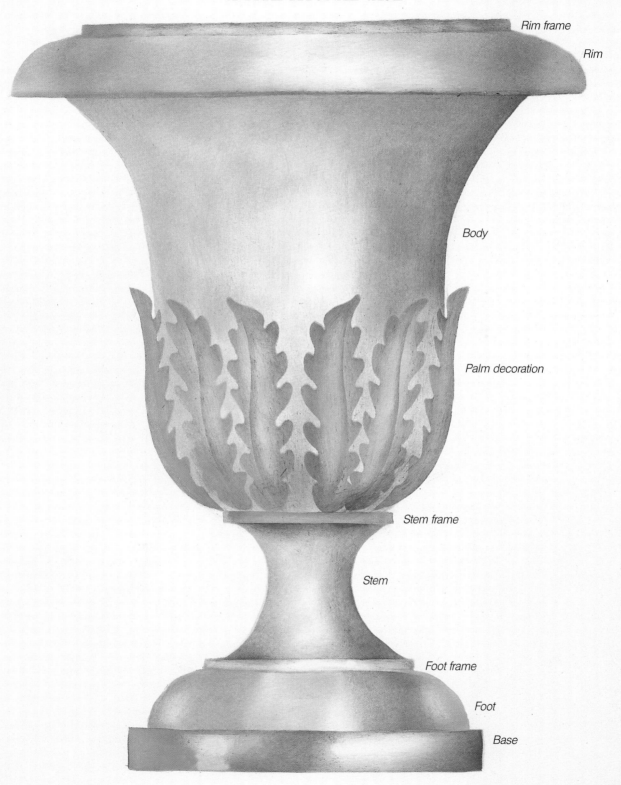

Rim frame

Rim

Body

Palm decoration

Stem frame

Stem

Foot frame

Foot

Base

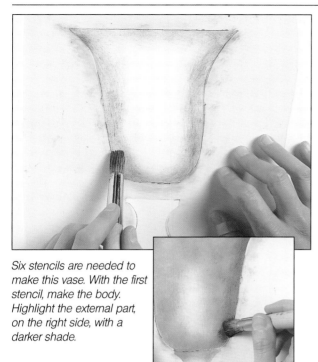

Six stencils are needed to make this vase. With the first stencil, make the body. Highlight the external part, on the right side, with a darker shade.

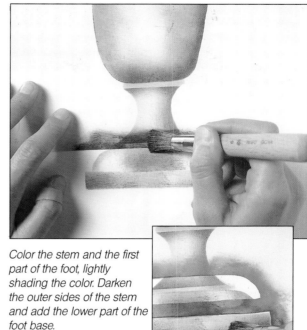

Color the stem and the first part of the foot, lightly shading the color. Darken the outer sides of the stem and add the lower part of the foot base.

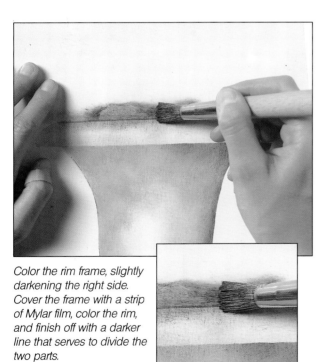

Color the rim frame, slightly darkening the right side. Cover the frame with a strip of Mylar film, color the rim, and finish off with a darker line that serves to divide the two parts.

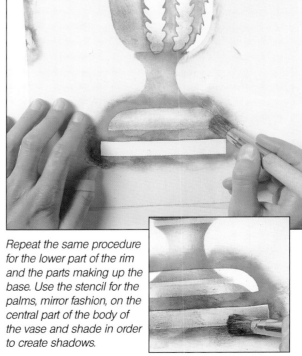

Repeat the same procedure for the lower part of the rim and the parts making up the base. Use the stencil for the palms, mirror fashion, on the central part of the body of the vase and shade in order to create shadows.

# WALL LAMP AND CANDLEHOLDER

*This three-branched candleholder is easy to make, although it does require a careful analysis of the elements and angles.*

Reality and imagination alternate in this composition: the two candleholders at the back are, in fact, faithful stencil reproductions of the original ones.

The black candleholder, with its sober line, can be divided into different parts: the foot, the body, the candleholder, and the candle. The original candleholder was of antique-style iron of a greenish color, rather difficult to copy. Green shades can be obtained by first coloring the object in emerald green and then applying a glazing of black over it. The foot of the candleholder is shaded in order to give it a volumetric effect.

Isolating the parts of the crude copper candleholder with grape decoration is slightly more complicated in that the object has elaborate, overlapping lines. The round base was made in three steps, staggering the surfaces.

The grapevine curling around the stem of the candleholder is purely pictorial.

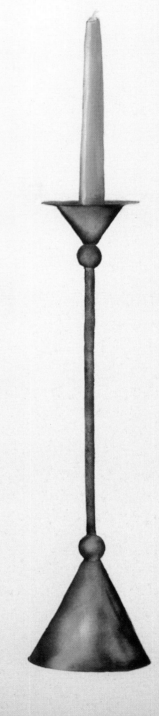

# PEWTER GOBLETS AND PLATES

A stencil paintbrush is indispensable when shading the glossy and reflecting surfaces of pewter objects. The shadows are delicately drawn according to the light's direction, in this case from in front.

The glass
The dark shadow in the center of the glass is reflected right down to the base. The right part is slightly darker, while a light gray tone prevails down the left side.

The goblet
This large, round goblet has the same dark shadings stretching from the center right down to the base. Two areas of light are visible to the left and right of the dark line.

The plate
This is made with a four-step stencil: one for the outline, two for the decoration, and one for the central part. A dark, sharp circle divides the center of the plate from its rim.

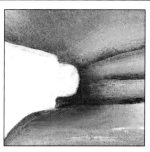
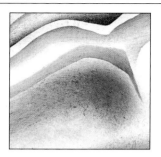
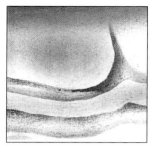

# CLOTHES HANGER

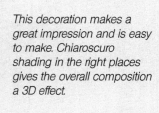

This decoration makes a great impression and is easy to make. Chiaroscuro shading in the right places gives the overall composition a 3D effect.

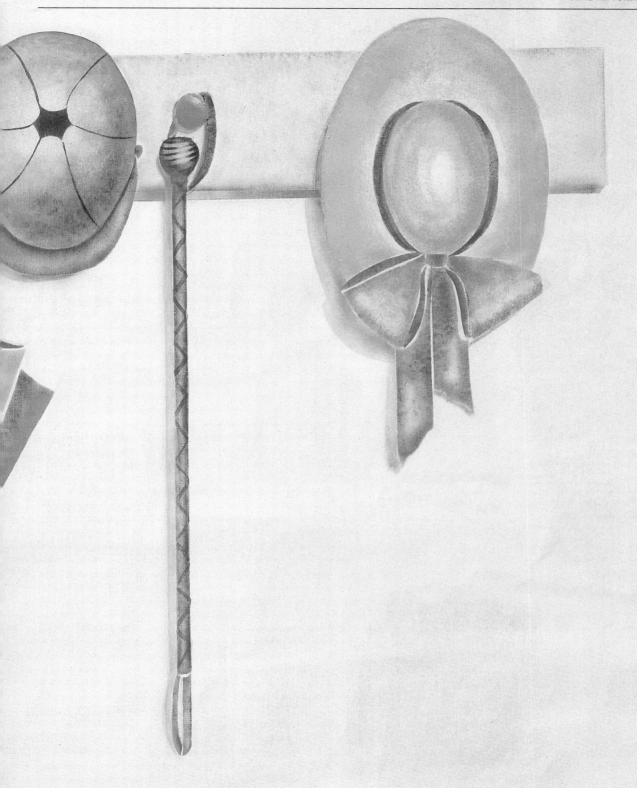

# STRAW HAT WITH RIBBON

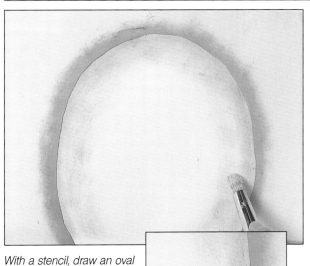

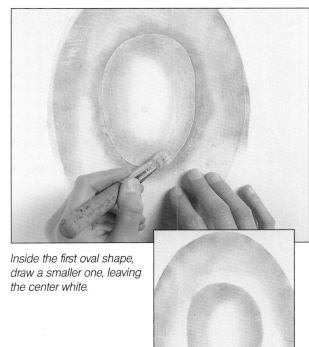

With a stencil, draw an oval shape the size of the hat. Coloring the stencil from the outside inwards, leave a space of about 10 cm at the bottom for the ribbon.

Inside the first oval shape, draw a smaller one, leaving the center white.

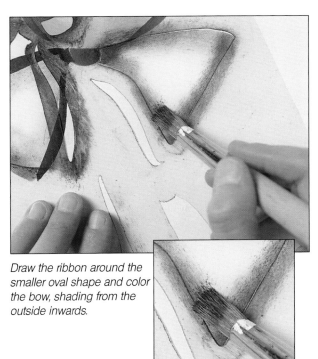

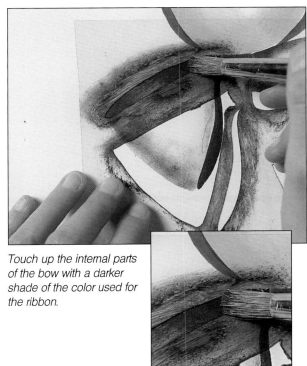

Draw the ribbon around the smaller oval shape and color the bow, shading from the outside inwards.

Touch up the internal parts of the bow with a darker shade of the color used for the ribbon.

# RIDING CAP AND CROP

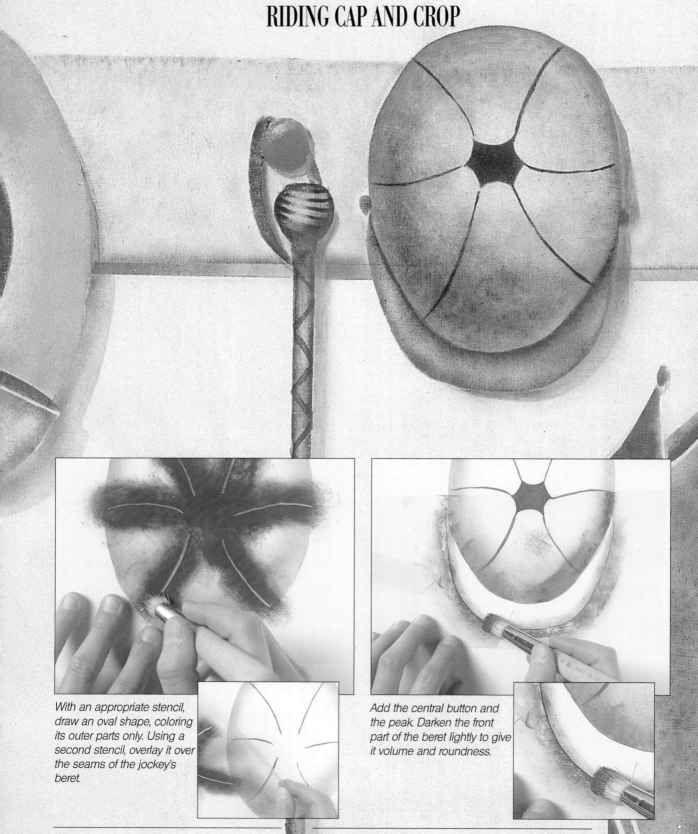

With an appropriate stencil, draw an oval shape, coloring its outer parts only. Using a second stencil, overlay it over the seams of the jockey's beret.

Add the central button and the peak. Darken the front part of the beret lightly to give it volume and roundness.

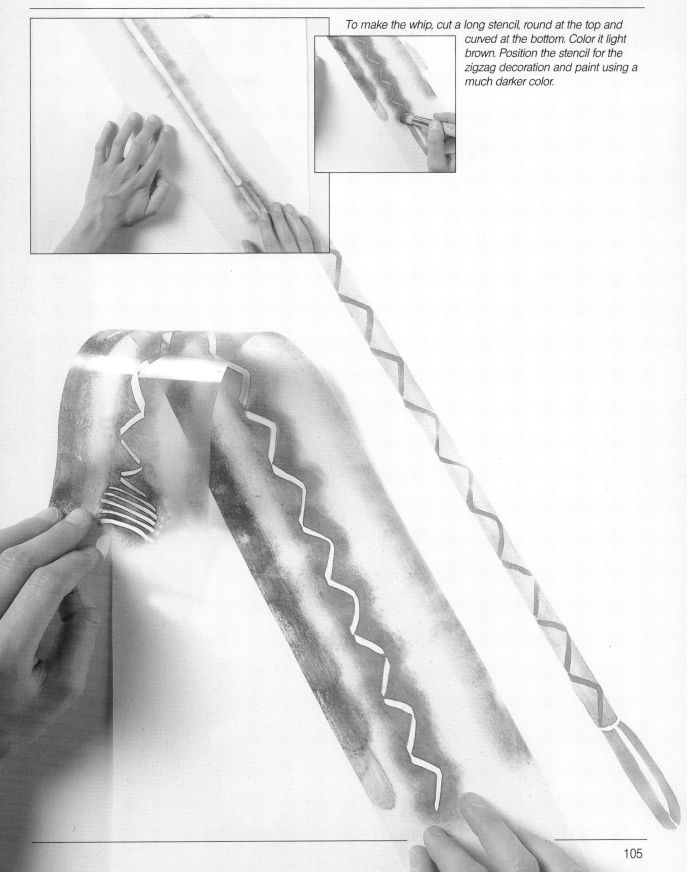

To make the whip, cut a long stencil, round at the top and curved at the bottom. Color it light brown. Position the stencil for the zigzag decoration and paint using a much darker color.

# AN UMBRELLA

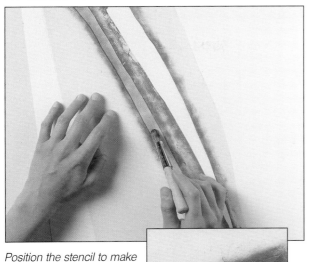

Position the stencil to make the folds on the left side, and then shift it in turn to make the remaining folds. Color the top part of the folds with a darker green.

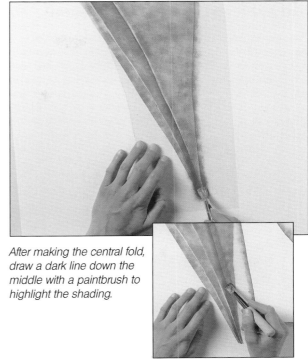

After making the central fold, draw a dark line down the middle with a paintbrush to highlight the shading.

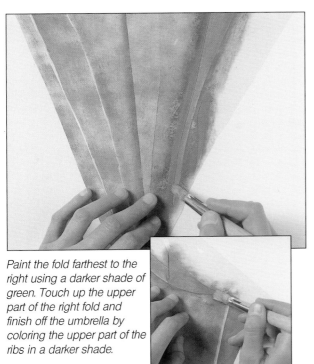

Paint the fold farthest to the right using a darker shade of green. Touch up the upper part of the right fold and finish off the umbrella by coloring the upper part of the ribs in a darker shade.

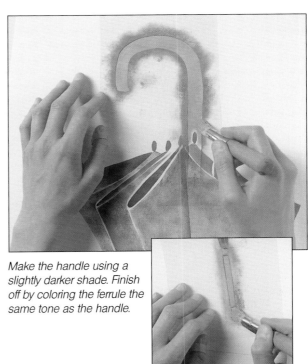

Make the handle using a slightly darker shade. Finish off by coloring the ferrule the same tone as the handle.

# CHINESE MOTIFS

*Transform an everyday lampshade into something special and refined. For this decoration, position the stencils, attaching them with* *repositionable spray. Use colors specifically designed for fabrics. To create the shadows, shade in various tones of blue.*

# "POTICHE"

*To create this Chinese vase, break up the picture into various elements and make the stencils: one for the outline, three for the rose decoration, and one for the lid.* *The shadows that underline the roundness of the vase are painted freehand in gray. The color is darker towards the vase and shaded towards the outside.*

# ARCHITECTONIC MOTIFS

By taking as our model the stucco work that decorated residential homes during the Regency and Victorian ages, we can create eye-catching, tone-on-tone stencils of great elegance.

## VICTORIAN MOTIF

This design, which reproduces a border from the Victorian age, is an example in which elements are isolated from the original design. As the motif is symmetrical, it is sufficient to trace the left side and fold the sheet in half to reproduce the right part, as in a mirror. Therefore, make two stencils, one for the brighter parts of the decoration (the base and the shell), the other for the shaded parts.

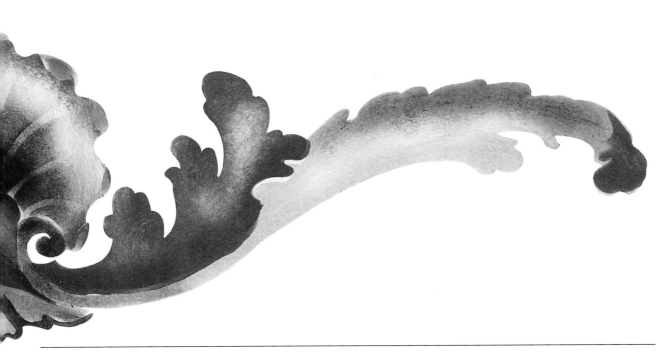

# THE CAPITAL

*This classical Ionic capital with its volutes and palm patterns is made with a four-step stencil. Begin by* *applying a very light coat of color, then continue with four tones of color to create the shading.*

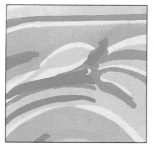

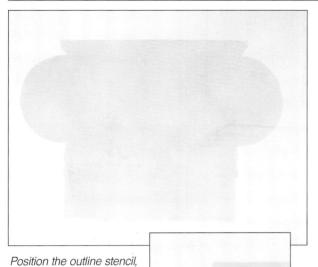

*Position the outline stencil, and coat lightly and uniformly with color.*

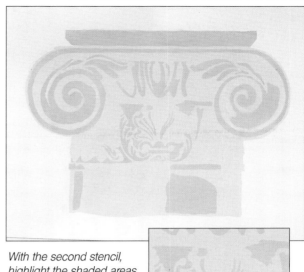

*With the second stencil, highlight the shaded areas by using a slightly darker shade of green than the previous one.*

*During the third step, by using a yet darker shade, the intermediate-shaded areas are made evident.*

*The last stencil brings out the very dark shades. A drop of black was added to make a green that was even more intense.*

# THE ROSE MOTIF

This rose motif with central flowers and a crown of oak leaves is made by overlaying four stencils, one for each shade of color.
This is a classic motif used as a center ceiling decoration or to enhance a coffer ceiling.

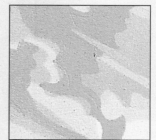

Position the first stencil and color with a very light tone in order to obtain a light, even base.

Apply the first shapes with the second stencil and shade each with a lighter tone than the previous one.

With the third stencil, highlight the parts that are slightly in the shade. Use a delicate color.

The fourth and last stencil completes the shading. The use of a decidedly darker tone brings out the composition shapes in sharp relief.

# STENCILS

# DOMENICHINO

# VERONA

# PERUGIA

# ASSISI

# CATHERINE

# ANASTASIA

# VATICAN

# FERRARA

# URBINO

# RENAISSANCE

# AREZZO

# ARMERINA

# VENICE

# IRAN

# SIENA

# EMPOLI

# MANTUA

# AOSTA

# ATHENS

# TREVISO

# PANAREA

# SOFIA

# SAINT DENIS

# VIENNA

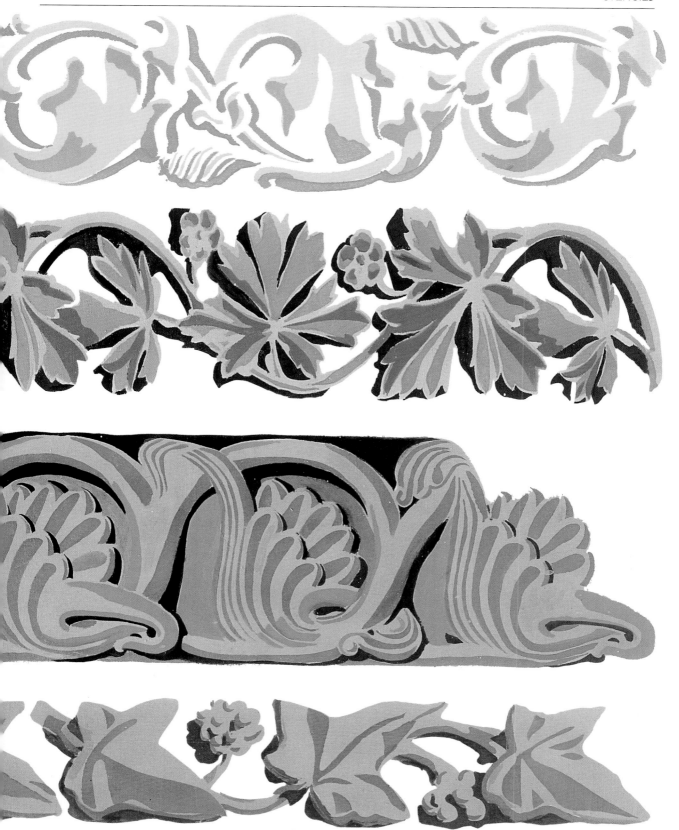

# VICENZA

# PARMA

# STROMBOLI

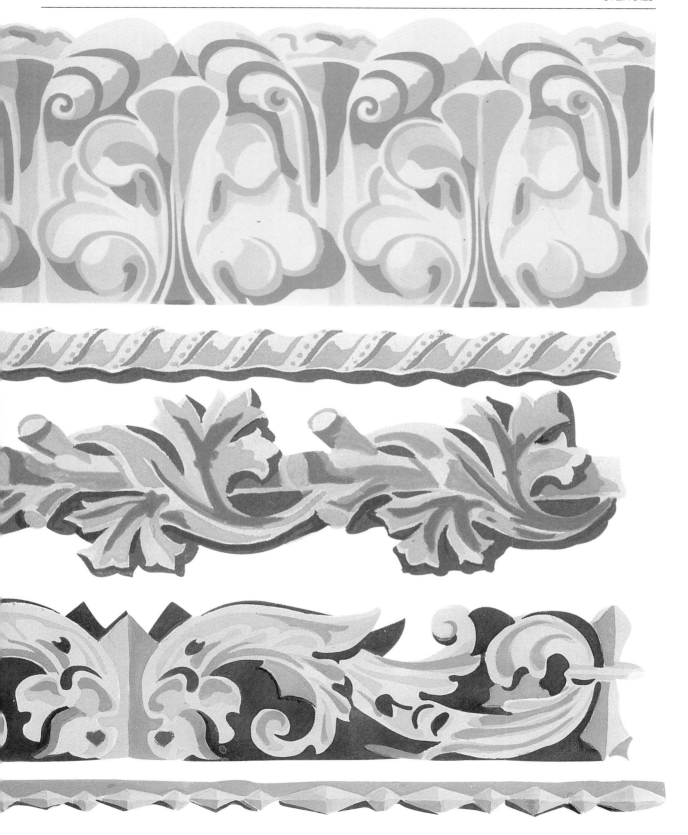

# BLUEBELLS

# VIOLETS

# LYLIUM

# FRUIT BOWL

# TEA SERVICE

# INDEX

Connie Parkinson, Indexer 614/ 866-0725
3-dimensional effects, 9, 74-77, 84, 100
3-D stencil, making, 56-83
acrylic colors, 8, 11
Anastasia, 128-129
Aosta, 142-143
Arezzo, 138-139
Armerina, 138-139
Assisi, 124-125
Athens, 144-145
Baroque, 31
Bluebells, 150-151
Bottle, 40
bridges, using, 22, 23, 24
bridges defined, 14
brushes, 9, 11, 16, 17, 98
    fine, 23-25, 42, 49, 57, 79
Candle, 66-67
Candleholder, 96-97
Cap, 101, 104
Catherine, 126-127
Cats, 53
chiaroscuro, 6, 9, 16, 34, 35, 39, 44,
    56, 57, 84, 100
circular strokes, 16, 64, 82
Classic rose, 114-115
Clothes hanger, 100-107
color gradation, 88-93
corners, 31
creating
    books, 93
    contours first, 16, 30
    frame, 91
curved stencil, 32-33
cutter, 11
cutting stencil, 15
Cyclamen and lylium, 83
depth in corners, 91
detailing. See touchup
Dogs, 52
Domenichino, 118-119
double-step stencil
    coloring, 30-31
    making, 28-29
Eagle, 17
Empoli, 142-143
Fan, 38-39
Ferrara, 9, 132-133

filling spaces, 23, 25, 57
flower parts, 25
Fried eggs and French bread,
    70-71
Fruit bowl, 156-157
Fruit in crystal bowl, 62-65
Glass, 98
Glass and jug, 68-69
Goblet, 98-99
Grapes, 50-51
highlighting, 24, 35, 45, 107, 115
intensifying colors, 97, 113
Ionic capital, 112-113
Iran, 140-141
isolating details, 18
isolating parts, 97
Ivy, 48-49
Lace and rose tray, 80-81
Liberty, 18, 19
light source, 6, 38-41, 47, 48, 49, 51,
    62-67, 84-87, 91, 98-99
lines and veins, stencils for, 47
liquid creams, 8, 11
Lotus, 16, 18, 19
Lylium, 154-155
Mantua, 142-143
motifs in sequence, 17
movement, illusion of, 9, 16, 17, 48
Mylar film, 11, 14, 47, 60, 93
Padova, 18, 19
painting on pottery, 11
Panarea, 146-147
paper adhesive, 11, 80, 91, 93
Parma, 148-149
Pears and cherries, 78-79
perspective, 6, 42, 56, 58-59, 60
Perugia, 20-21, 122-123
Pewter goblets and plates, 98-99
Plate, 99
positioning/repositioning, 33, 35, 45,
    46, 49, 51, 87, 107
Potiche, 108
Ramage, 42-43
reference points, 34-35
Renaissance, 136-137
repeating the design, 15
repositionable spray, 11, 80, 108
retarding medium, 8-9, 11, 64
Rhombi box, 86-87

rollers, 9, 11, 34-35
Rose vine, 42-43
Rovigo, 18, 19
Saint Denis, 146-147
Satin shoe, 41
separating elements, 20, 45, 96
shadows, 74, 84-85
Shelf, 58-61
Shells and lobster, 74-77
Siena, 140-141
Siracusa, 32-33
Sofia, 146-147
Spoleto, 28-29
spray paint, transparent, 80
stencil friezes, 15, 16, 17, 18
stenciling
    on fabric, 11
    on pottery. See painting
Still life, 57
Straw hat with ribbon, 101, 102-103
Stromboli, 148-149
stucco motifs patterns, 110-116
Tea Service, 158-159
Theorem rose, 44-47
touchup, 25, 42, 52, 53, 56, 64,
    77, 103
tracing design outlines, 15
tracing paper, 28, 29
transparency, illusion of, 40,
    64-65, 82
Trasimeno, 30
Treviso, 144-145
trompe l'oeil, 6, 38, 42, 44, 52, 56
Umbrella, 100-101, 106-107
Urbino, 134-135
vase, traditional, parts, 94
Vatican, 130-131
veins and branches, 23, 42, 44, 79,
    80-81
Venice, 138-139
Verona, 19, 21, 120-121
Vicenza, 148-149
Victorian motif, 110-111
Vienna, 146-147
Violets, 152-153
volume, illusion of, 6, 16, 42, 56, 58-59,
    60, 71, 72-73, 97
Wall lamp, 96
Whip, 101, 104-105